Cuba

JOY GREGORY

MEDIA ENHANCED BOOKS
AV² BY WEIGL™
ADDED VALUE · AUDIO VISUAL

www.av2books.com

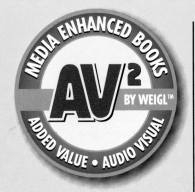

AV² provides enriched content that supplements and complements this book. Weigl's AV² books strive to create inspired learning and engage young minds in a total learning experience.

Your AV² Media Enhanced books come alive with...

Audio
Listen to sections of the book read aloud.

Key Words
Study vocabulary, and complete a matching word activity.

Video
Watch informative video clips.

Quizzes
Test your knowledge.

Go to www.av2books.com, and enter this book's unique code.

BOOK CODE

B 3 9 6 3 4 6

Embedded Weblinks
Gain additional information for research.

Slide Show
View images and captions, and prepare a presentation.

AV² by Weigl brings you media enhanced books that support active learning.

Try This!
Complete activities and hands-on experiments.

... and much, much more!

Published by AV² by Weigl
350 5th Avenue, 59th Floor
New York, NY 10118
Website: www.av2books.com

Library of Congress Cataloging-in-Publication Data

Names: Gregory, Joy, author.
  Title: Cuba / Joy Gregory.
  Description: New York, NY : AV2 by Weigl, 2016. | Series: Exploring countries
    | Includes index.
  Identifiers: LCCN 2015049787 (print) | LCCN 2015050077 (ebook) | ISBN
    9781489646057 (hard cover : alk. paper) | ISBN 9781489650245 (soft cover :
    alk. paper) | ISBN 9781489646064 (Multi-User eBook)
  Subjects: LCSH: Cuba—Juvenile literature. | Cuba—Description and
    travel--Juvenile literature.
  Classification: LCC F1758.5 .G73 2016 (print) | LCC F1758.5 (ebook) | DDC
    972.91—dc23

Printed in the United States of America in Brainerd, Minnesota
1 2 3 4 5 6 7 8 9 20 19 18 17 16

032016
150316

Project Coordinator Heather Kissock
Art Director Terry Paulhus

Photo Credits
Every reasonable effort has been made to trace ownership and to obtain permission to reprint copyright material. The publishers would be pleased to have any errors or omissions brought to their attention so that they may be corrected in subsequent printings.

Weigl acknowledges Corbis Images, Getty Images, Alamy, and Newscom as its primary photo suppliers for this title.

Contents

Cuba Overview

Cuba is an island nation in North America. It is located where the Atlantic Ocean, Gulf of Mexico, and Caribbean Sea meet. Indians from South America or Florida first settled Cuba. In 1492, Christopher Columbus landed there and claimed the area for Spain. Cuba was a Spanish **colony** until 1898. In 1959, Fidel Castro and his rebel soldiers defeated the Cuban president and his army. Cuba soon became a **communist** country. Many Cubans are poor, but the communist government has improved education and health care.

The Malecon is an avenue along the water in Havana. If offers a view of the city's mix of colorful new and older buildings.

Cubans celebrate the May Day holiday on May 1 with parades featuring large photos of Fidel Castro.

American cars from the 1950s are a common sight in Cuba. It has been illegal to send U.S. cars to the country since the early 1960s.

The royal palm is the national tree of Cuba. It can grow from 50 to 75 feet (15 to 23 meters) tall.

More than 500 types of fish live in the waters around Cuba.

Exploring Cuba

Cuba is located about 90 miles (150 kilometers) south of Florida. The country includes a large main island and more than 1,600 other islands, **islets**, and **cays**. Cuba covers a total area of 42,390 square miles (109,820 square kilometers). It is slightly smaller than the state of Pennsylvania. Cuba's coastline is about 3,570 miles (5,745 km) long. Beaches, **mangrove** swamps, and coral reefs line the coast. The main island, also called Cuba, is the largest island in the Caribbean region. It is 777 miles (1,250 km) long. The island ranges in width from 19 miles (31 km) to 119 miles (191 km).

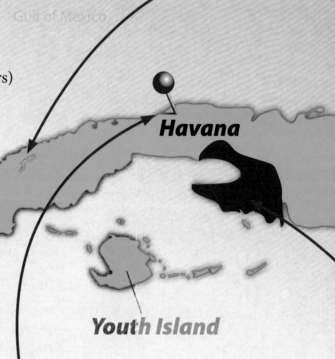

UNITED STATES (Florida)

Gulf of Mexico

Straits of Florida

Havana

Youth Island

Caribbean Sea

Cayman Islands

N

Havana

Map Legend

Cuba	▲▲▲ Sierra Maestra	Viñales Valley
Land	Capital City	
Water	Zapata Swamp	SCALE

SCALE 50 Miles

50 Kilometers

Viñales Valley

The Viñales Valley is located in western Cuba. Tall, rounded hills rise from the flat valley. For centuries, farmers have grown tobacco in the area. **UNESCO** has named it a World Heritage Site.

The Bahamas

Viñales Valley

CUBA

Sierra Maestra

Zapata Swamp

Jamaica

Haiti

Havana

Havana is the capital of Cuba. The city was founded in 1519 on a bay where ships could dock easily. This feature has made Havana a major port city.

Zapata Swamp

Zapata Swamp is the country's largest wetland area. Four kinds of mangroves grow in this swamp. It provides a home to half of the bird **species** in Cuba.

Sierra Maestra

The Sierra Maestra is Cuba's largest mountain range. It is located on the southeastern part of the main island. The Sierra Maestra is home to many kinds of plants and animals.

LAND AND CLIMATE

Plains and low hills cover about two-thirds of the island of Cuba. Much of the remaining land is mountainous. Most mountains are found along the coastline. The Sierra Maestra range includes Turquino Peak, the highest peak in Cuba.

Hundreds of rivers and streams flow through the island of Cuba. Most are shallow and carry very little water. The Cauto River in eastern Cuba is the country's longest river.

Many of Cuba's lakes also are shallow. The country's largest lake is Laguna de la Leche, or "Milk Lagoon." Channels of water connect Laguna de la Leche to the sea. Sometimes, seawater flows inland and stirs **minerals** at the bottom of the lake. This action produces the lake's milky color.

Waterfalls are a common feature of Cuba's mountain rivers and streams.

The land on Youth Island, Cuba's second-largest island, varies widely. It changes from sand and clay plains in the north to a large area covered by gravel in the south. The northwestern and southeastern parts of the island are hilly, and trees cover these hills.

Cuba is located in the region of Earth near the **equator** called the tropics. In tropical countries such as Cuba, the weather is warm year-round. The rainiest months of the year in Cuba are May through October. These are also the country's warmest months. In August, the average temperature is 82° Fahrenheit (28° Celsius). In January, the average is 73°F (23°C).

Hurricanes often strike Cuba. These tropical storms with high winds and heavy rains most often occur from June to November. They can cause a great deal of damage. In 1932, a powerful hurricane caused the death of more than 3,000 people. To help people prepare for future hurricanes, the government set up a warning system to alert residents when a storm is approaching.

The Sierra del Escambray mountain range rises behind the Valley de los Ingenios on the island of Cuba. The range's highest mountain is 3,740 feet (1,140 m) tall.

54 INCHES
Average amount of rainfall each year. (137 centimeters)

230 **Miles** Length of the Cauto River. (370 km)

6,476 Feet Height of Turquino Peak. (1,974 m)

150 MILES
Length of the Sierra Maestra mountain range. (240 km)

PLANTS AND ANIMALS

Cuba is home to a number of endemic plant and animal species. Endemic species are those found only in certain areas and nowhere else. Several thousand kinds of flowering plants grow only in Cuba. Endemic species of palm trees and cacti also are found there. When large areas of land were cleared for farming, much of the main island's native plant life was destroyed. However, in the 1960s, the government began to replant forests. Trees now cover about 25 percent of the island.

Several species of birds, **mammals**, **reptiles**, **amphibians**, and fish are endemic to the country. The bee hummingbird is the world's smallest bird and is only the size of a large bee. Other endemic species include several kinds of bats and reptiles such as the Cuban crocodile. More than 60 species of frogs and toads live only in Cuba. One kind of freshwater fish lives only on Youth Island, which used to be called the Isle of Pines. The fish is named the Isle of Pines Rivulus.

Cuban crocodiles live only in the Zapata Swamp and on Youth Island. They can grow up to 10.5 feet (3.2 m) long.

Plants and Animals BY THE NUMBERS

More Than 7,000
Number of insect species in Cuba.

5 FEET Length of the green stems produced by the mariposa flower. (1.5 m)

2–2.5 INCHES
Length of the bee hummingbird. (5.5–6 cm)

5 to 10 Years
Average life of a Cuban tree frog.

NATURAL RESOURCES

Fertile soil is one of Cuba's most important natural resources. Crops can grow on about one-third of the land. In some areas, farmers can raise two crops each year. Cuba produces sugarcane and tobacco for **export**. Farmers also grow rice, coffee, beans, vegetables, and fruits.

Cuba's forests are another natural resource. Wood from pine trees is burned for fuel. Mahogany trees have a dark wood that is used to make furniture. Sometimes, mahogany is also used in buildings. Black piano keys and parts of furniture are made from the wood of ebony trees.

Fishing boats catch tuna, hake, and needlefish. Cubans also raise large numbers of fish in ponds and tanks. These aquaculture farms produce sea bass, tilapia, and carp.

Cuba has one of the world's largest **reserves** of nickel ore. Nickel is often used to coat and protect other metals. Natural resources mined in Cuba also include iron ore, copper, manganese, and salt.

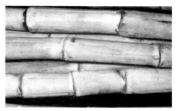

1st Sugarcane's rank among the largest crops grown in Cuba.

33,000 TONS
Amount of fish produced in a year by Cuba's aquaculture farms. (30,000 metric tons)

5.5 Million Tons
Size of Cuba's nickel reserves. (5 million metric tons)

Farmers often use oxen instead of tractors to plow their fields. Gasoline to fuel tractors is in short supply in Cuba.

TOURISM

About 3 million tourists visited Cuba in 2014, the highest number in the country's history. Many tourists spend time on Cuba's white-sand beaches. Others enjoy diving, snorkeling, or fishing in the blue-green waters that surround Cuba.

Varadero is one of Cuba's most popular beaches. It is located on the northern coast of the main island. Divers can also explore a nearby underwater park, where ships have been sunk to create homes for fish. Hikers enjoy the variety of plants and animals in Hicacos Point Natural Park, which is close to Varadero.

Some of Cuba's smaller islands also receive many visitors. Cayo Coco is home to more than 200 species of birds. Paradise Beach is on the island of Cayo Largo del Sur. Calm, shallow waters make it popular with swimmers.

The mangrove jellyfish, which often lives upside down in shallow water along Cuba's coast, is one of many kinds of sea life attracting divers and snorkelers.

Cayo Coco is part of a group of islands called King's Gardens that feature lush plant life as well as peaceful beaches.

People visit El Baba Nature Park to see its birds, turtles, and crocodiles. Tourists can also learn about Cuban culture at the park. Those who want to learn about Cuba's history can visit the country's UNESCO World Heritage Sites. One site includes the city of Trinidad and the nearby Valley de los Ingenios. *Ingenios* means "sugar mills." During the late 18th century, the sugar industry became important in the area. The UNESCO site has historic homes and former sugar mills.

The Old Havana section of the capital city is another popular tourist destination. Visitors walk its **cobblestone** streets and nine plazas, or public squares. Many of the homes and other buildings found here were put up when Cuba was a colony and show the influence of Spanish **architecture**.

Another popular UNESCO site is San Pedro de la Roca Castle. Spain built this fort in the 17th century to protect the harbor in the city of Santiago de Cuba. It is one of the best examples of Spanish forts in the Americas.

For many years after Fidel Castro became Cuba's leader, the U.S. government did not permit most American tourists to visit Cuba. Recently, more Americans are being allowed to travel there. They must state that their visit is for an educational or other special purpose.

Tourism BY THE NUMBERS

MORE THAN 100
Number of nature and hiking trails in Cuba.

1638 Year San Pedro de la Roca Castle was completed.

9 Number of Cuba's UNESCO World Heritage Sites.

2015 Year when the U.S. government began to make it easier for Americans to travel to Cuba.

A former church in Trinidad is now one of the city's many museums. Visitors can climb the bell tower for a view of the city.

INDUSTRY

C uba's communist government controls most farms, factories, and other businesses. It decides which products are made and how much will be made. Profits go to the government, which pays the workers. However, since 2011, the government has been allowing some people to own businesses.

Mining and oil production are important industries in Cuba. The country has oil reserves of about 124 million **barrels**, and it produces about 50,000 barrels of oil per day. Products manufactured in the country include steel, cement, farm machinery, and medicines. Cuban workers also produce refrigerators, cell phones, beverages, clothing, and furniture.

Besides wood and oil, Cuba uses peat for fuel. Peat is plant material that has rotted in water. It is dried and then burned. Sugarcane is also burned in some power plants to make electricity. In southeastern Cuba, dams have been built on rivers to produce **hydroelectricity**.

72% Percentage of workers employed by the government.

28% Portion of Cubans working in industry or agriculture.

4 Number of refineries in Cuba that turn oil into products such as gasoline and heating fuel.

303,100 Tons
Amount of salt mined in Cuba each year. (275,000 metric tons)

Government-owned factories produce most of the clothing made in Cuba.

GOODS AND SERVICES

Cuba's farmers, miners, and factory workers do not produce enough goods to meet the country's needs. Cuba must **import** many types of products. These include oil, machinery, chemicals, rice, and other foods.

Often, imported food is expensive. The government **subsidizes** the cost of some food products. It also rations basic food items, or limits the amounts people can buy. Rationed items include eggs, milk, chicken, and beans.

The countries that a nation exports goods to and imports goods from are called its trading partners. Cuba's largest trading partners include Venezuela, China, Canada, and Spain. The U.S. government does not allow most types of goods to be sold to or bought from Cuba.

About 72 percent of workers in Cuba have service jobs. These people provide a service to others rather than produce goods. Service workers include tour guides, teachers, doctors, and nurses. Cuba sends many doctors to work in Venezuela. In exchange, Venezuela provides Cuba with oil.

$15 Billion Value of the goods Cuba imports each year.

ALMOST 40% Portion of Cuba's imports that come from Venezuela.

1961 Year that the U.S. Congress passed a law stopping trade with Cuba.

The Cuban government has started to let people open their own restaurants. The food servers and cooks are service workers.

INDIGENOUS PEOPLES

By the late 1400s, several groups of **indigenous** people lived in Cuba. Scientists believe the Guanahatabey and Ciboney people settled in Cuba in about 4000 BC. They hunted animals and gathered plants for food. The Ciboney people lived in small communities of one or two families. Some groups lived in caves.

Many scientists think that the Taino came to Cuba from South America around AD 500. They relied on the fish and fruit found in Cuba, while also growing corn, beans, and root crops, such as potatoes and manioc. The Taino lived in large settlements. Their homes were made mostly of mud and plants.

The Taino built canoes strong enough to use in the ocean. They made pottery and used dyed cotton thread to make cloth. The Taino also played games with a rubber ball. They later introduced those games to Spanish settlers.

3,000
Number of people living in some Taino communities.

75,000 Total number of indigenous people living in Cuba by the 15th century.

10 Fewest number of players on a team in Taino ball games, which were played on a court shaped like a rectangle.

Re-created Taino houses can be seen today at the Chorro de Maita museum near the town of Banes.

THE AGE OF EXPLORATION

Christopher Columbus sailed from Spain with three ships in 1492 to look for a sea route to India and other parts of Asia. Soon after he reached Cuba, more Spanish ships arrived. By 1511, Spanish settlers had formed a small community on the northeastern coast of Cuba.

Spain soon took control of all of Cuba. Settlers brought Spanish customs and the Roman Catholic religion to the colony. They took land from the indigenous people, whom they called Indians. Spanish settlers started to bring African slaves to Cuba.

Less than 50 years after the Spanish took control of Cuba, only a small number of indigenous people were alive. Some had died fighting the Spanish or had starved to death after losing their land. European diseases had killed many others. Some of the remaining indigenous people married Spanish settlers or African slaves. By the late 1500s, many of Cuba's people had a mixed Spanish, African, and Indian background.

300 Number of people at the Baracoa settlement in northeast Cuba in 1511.

ABOUT 3,000 Number of indigenous people in the mid-1500s.

1553 Year that Havana became Cuba's capital.

Christopher Columbus landed on the northern shore of Cuba on October 28, 1492. He named the island Juana, in honor of a child of the king and queen of Spain.

EARLY SETTLERS

Spain divided Cuba into seven political districts. Each district had its own council, or local government. The councils controlled the land in their area. They forced indigenous people to work for the Spanish and **convert** to the Catholic faith.

The Spanish found gold in Cuba, and many of the first settlers hoped to get rich quickly by mining gold. A large portion of the slaves brought to Cuba in the colony's early years were forced to work in gold mines. However, there was actually little gold in Cuba. Settlers then established sugar, coffee, and tobacco **plantations**, and they used slaves to work in the fields.

Over the years, Cuba's population increased, including the number of slaves. By the 1840s, slaves made up about one-third of the population. Slavery did not become illegal in Cuba until 1886.

Today's sugarcane workers use a broad, heavy knife, called a machete, to cut the thick stems. Slaves used this same tool in the 18th and 19th centuries.

Plantation owners lived in large homes called haciendas. Some of them can still be seen in Cuba today.

By the mid-1800s, many Cubans wanted to be free of Spanish rule. Some large landowners had become very wealthy, but most farmers and other workers were poor. From 1868 to 1878, Cubans fought a war of independence against Spain that was called the Ten Years' War. Spain won the Ten Year's War and kept control.

In 1898, the Spanish-American War between Spain and the United States ended Spain's control over Cuba. However, Cuba did not become fully independent at once. The United States had sent troops to Cuba to fight the Spanish. After the war, U.S. soldiers stayed in Cuba. They helped build bridges, schools, and roads. In addition, U.S. generals played a major role in running the government, although this was unpopular with many Cubans. In 1902, most U.S. troops left Cuba, and an elected Cuban president took office. However, a U.S.-Cuban agreement allowed the United States to keep a military base at Guantánamo Bay.

Early Settlers BY THE NUMBERS

About 1.3 Million
Number of people who lived in Cuba by 1860.

200,000 Number of
lives lost in the Ten Years' War.

45 Square Miles
Size of the U.S. military base at Guantánamo Bay. (116 sq. km)

The Spanish-American War began after the U.S. battleship *Maine* exploded in Havana's harbor. The U.S. government blamed Spain for the loss of the ship.

POPULATION

More than 11 million people live in Cuba. With a population of 2.1 million, Havana is Cuba's largest city. More than three-quarters of the country's population lives in cities or towns.

Life expectancy in Cuba is high. On average, men can expect to live to age 76 and women to nearly 81 years old. These long lives are partly due to the country's good health-care system.

The population has been growing slowly or not at all in recent years. One reason is that many families have few children. Cuba's birth rate, the number of children born per 1,000 people, is less than 10. This figure is lower than the birth rate of almost every other country in the world. In addition, many Cubans have **emigrated** to the United States. About 700,000 left in the first few years after Fidel Castro became Cuba's leader. Since 1980, about 500,000 Cubans have come to the United States.

Children between the ages of 6 and 11 must attend school. About 86 percent of students go on to high school.

16% Portion of Cubans under the age of 15.

About 2 Million

Number of people in the United States who were born in Cuba or whose **ancestors** came from Cuba.

70% Portion of Cuban Americans who live in Florida.

POLITICS AND GOVERNMENT

For most of the 1950s, President Fulgencio Batista ruled Cuba as a **dictator**. He took government money and helped a few other Cubans become rich. He also helped U.S. and other foreign companies that owned land and businesses in Cuba. Most Cubans were very poor. After Fidel Castro removed Batista from office, he became Cuba's leader, remaining in that position from 1959 to 2008. Castro's government took over Cuban banks and businesses, including those owned by foreigners.

In 1976, Cuba adopted its current **constitution**. This document says that all power belongs to the people. However, the Communist Party is the only political party allowed in Cuba, and its leaders run the country.

The National Assembly of People's Power is Cuba's legislature and can pass laws. Members are elected, and they must belong to the Communist Party. The National Assembly meets for a short time twice each year.

The National Assembly chooses the country's president and 30 other members of the Council of State. The president is head of the Council of State. This group passes laws when the National Assembly is not meeting.

75% Portion of Cuban farmland owned by Americans and other non-Cubans before Fidel Castro took power in 1959.

614 Number of members in the National Assembly of People's Power.

2008

Year the National Assembly appointed Raúl Castro, Fidel Castro's brother, as president.

The National Assembly of People's Power must approve any changes to Cuba's constitution.

CULTURAL GROUPS

Spanish is the official language of Cuba, although some Cuban words can be traced to indigenous languages. For example, *hamaca* means "hammock," and *barbacoa* means "barbecue." Both words come from the language of the Taino people. The African languages of slaves added other words to Cuban Spanish.

The word *calle*, which means "street" in Spanish, appears on signs throughout Cuba.

The Spanish tradition of celebrating *quinceañera*, or a girl's 15th birthday, is very popular in Cuba. Many Cuban families save money for years in order to pay for their daughter's *quinceañera* celebration. The event often includes a fancy dress and large party.

Teenagers enjoy dancing at most *quinceañera* parties.

For centuries, Roman Catholicism was the main religion. Starting in 1959, the communist government limited religious freedom. Catholics were not allowed to be members of the Communist Party. However, in recent years, the government has allowed more religious liberty. It has also permitted visits to Cuba by the pope, or worldwide leader of the Roman Catholic Church.

Slaves brought their religions from Africa. Over time, beliefs and practices from African faiths and Roman Catholicism combined. An Afro-Cuban religion called Santería developed, and it is still practiced by many Cubans today. People who believe in Santería pray to Catholic saints as well as to African gods.

Traditional Cuban foods have become popular in many countries. Cuban cooks often flavor their food with sofrito. To make sofrito, they cook onion, green pepper, garlic, oregano, and ground black pepper in olive oil. Cuban recipes use sofrito in pork, chicken, and rice dishes.

Cultural Groups BY THE NUMBERS

2016 Year work began to build the first new Catholic church in Cuba since 1959.

50% OR MORE Portion of Cubans who practice the religion Santería.

Pope Francis was greeted by large crowds when he visited Cuba in 2015.

ARTS AND ENTERTAINMENT

T he government's Ministry of Culture supports the development of Cuban art. It supplies artists with the materials they need to produce their artworks. The ministry also makes sure that students who graduate from the country's leading art school have jobs.

Art galleries and museums feature the work of many Cuban artists, such as Rene Portocarrero. In the 20th century, he drew pictures of women in tropical settings and created artworks based on old buildings in Havana. Painter and photographer Raúl Martínez also worked in the 20th century. His art includes pictures of Cuban heroes and leaders.

Doves stand for the idea of peace in Rene Portocarrero's drawings, as well as in the work of many other artists.

Huge murals, or wall paintings, appear on the outside of buildings throughout Cuba.

Over the years, Cuba has developed several styles of dance and music. These include the rumba and salsa dances. Both use quick steps to a beat that started in the Afro-Cuban community. The *danzón* is another dance that began in Cuba. It draws on European traditions of ballroom dance. Cuba is also known for a style of Afro-Cuban jazz.

Ballet is popular in Cuba. Alicia Alonso is one of the country's best-known ballet dancers. In 1948, she started the dance group that became the National Ballet of Cuba. Many other Cuban dance companies perform modern and traditional types of dance.

Plays are performed in theaters around the country. Havana's National Theater of Cuba building includes two large auditoriums. Ballets as well as plays are performed there. Many cities have children's theaters.

Cuba's government supports the country's film industry. The Cuban Institute of Cinematographic Art and Industry produces many types of movies. It also sponsors the region's biggest film festival, the International Festival of New Latin American Cinema.

The Buena Vista Social Club, a Cuban band, performs around the world. The band's music is a mix of African and Cuban jazz.

3,500 Total number of seats in the two auditoriums of the National Theater of Cuba.

1971 Year that Cuba's second ballet company was started, in the city of Camagüey.

1978 Year that the first International Festival of New Latin American Cinema was held.

2 Number of national television stations in Cuba.

SPORTS

aseball is Cuba's most popular sport. It is called *la pelota*. In the 1860s, sailors and traders introduced the game to Cubans. The National Institute of Sports, Physical Education, and Recreation controls baseball and most other sports in Cuba. The institute organizes baseball leagues and national teams. The national teams take part in international competitions. Many Cubans who are not on organized teams also play baseball for fun.

Cuban players have been moving to the United States to play baseball since the 19th century. After 1959, the government stopped Cuban athletes, including baseball players, from joining U.S. professional teams. This meant that Cuban athletes could not receive the higher salaries professionals are paid in the United States. In recent decades, Cuban players wishing to join Major League Baseball (MLB) teams in the United States have had to emigrate without permission from the government. In 2016, MLB and Cuban government officials were discussing ways to make it easier for Cuban athletes to play in the United States.

Yoenis Céspedes left Cuba in 2011 to continue his baseball career in the United States. He played for the New York Mets in the 2015 World Series.

Strong pitching by Norberto Gonzalez helped Cuba's team win the gold medal for baseball at the 2004 Olympics in Athens, Greece.

Cuban boxers have earned worldwide success. Cuba's first world champion lightweight boxer was Esteban Bellán. Nicknamed "Kid Chocolate," he won the boxing title in 1931.

At the Olympics, boxers from Cuba have won more gold medals than fighters from any other country except the United States. Cuban athletes have also won medals in a number of other Olympic sports. These include judo, wrestling, weightlifting, and track and field events.

The government encourages all Cubans to play sports. It provides money for many different school and community youth programs. Almost all children have a chance to play games such as baseball, volleyball, and basketball. The government also helps the best young athletes prepare for international competitions. It provides these athletes with equipment and training.

Yarisley Silva won the silver medal in pole vaulting at the 2012 Olympics in London, Great Britain. She cleared the bar set at 15.6 feet (4.75 m).

Mapping Cuba

We use many tools to interpret maps and to understand the locations of features such as cities, states, lakes, and rivers. The map below has many tools to help interpret information on the map of Cuba.

Map of Cuba

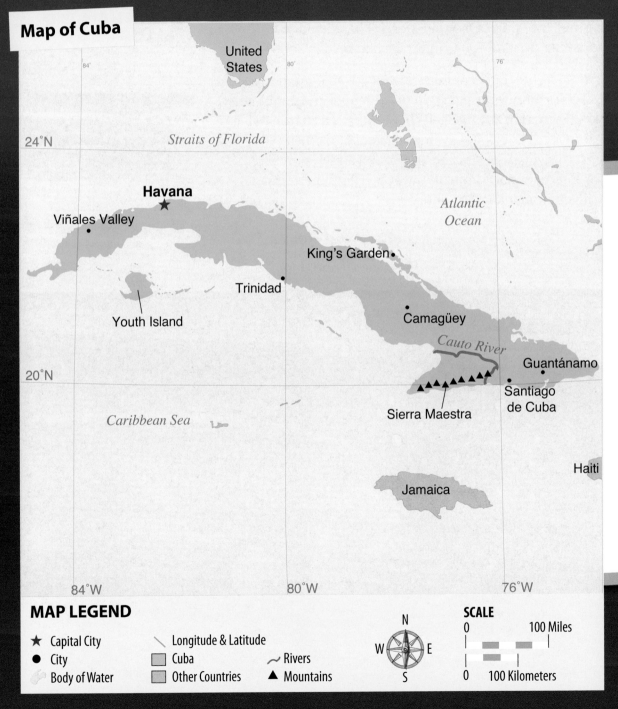

United States

84°

80°

76°

24°N

Straits of Florida

Havana ★

Viñales Valley •

Atlantic Ocean

King's Garden •

Trinidad •

Youth Island

Camagüey •

Cauto River

20°N

Guantánamo •

Sierra Maestra

Santiago de Cuba •

Caribbean Sea

Haiti

Jamaica

84°W

80°W

76°W

MAP LEGEND

★ Capital City
● City
🌊 Body of Water

╲ Longitude & Latitude
▢ Cuba
▢ Other Countries

〜 Rivers
▲ Mountains

N W E S

SCALE

0 ———— 100 Miles

0 ———— 100 Kilometers

Mapping Tools

- The compass rose shows north, south, east, and west. The points in between represent northeast, northwest, southeast, and southwest.
- The map scale shows that the distances on a map represent much longer distances in real life. If you measure the distance between objects on a map, you can use the map scale to calculate the actual distance in miles or kilometers between those two points.
- The lines of latitude and longitude are long lines that appear on maps. The lines of latitude run east to west and measure how far north or south of the equator a place is located. The lines of longitude run north to south and measure how far east or west of the Prime Meridian a place is located. A location on a map can be found by using the two numbers where latitude and longitude meet. This number is called a coordinate and is written using degrees and direction. For example, the city of Havana would be found at 23°N and 82°W on a map.

Map It!

Using the map and the appropriate tools, complete the activities below.

Locating with latitude and longitude
1. Which city is found at 22°N and 80°W?
2. What island is at 22°N and 83°W?
3. Which large city is found at 20°N and 76°W?

Distances between points
4. Using the map scale and a ruler, calculate the approximate distance between the cities of Havana and Santiago de Cuba.
5. What is the approximate distance from Trinidad in the middle of Cuba to Guantánamo on the eastern side?
6. What is the approximate distance between Camagüey and Guantánamo?

Quiz Time

Test your knowledge of Cuba by answering these questions.

1 Which ocean is to the east of Cuba?

2 What is the longest river in Cuba?

3 What is the name of the highest mountain in Cuba?

4 What is Cuba's largest crop?

5 What is the largest city in Cuba?

6 Who became president of Cuba in 2008?

7 What group of indigenous people came to Cuba around AD 500?

8 What year did Spain's control of Cuba end?

9 Who won Cuba's first lightweight boxing title in 1931?

10 What is Cuba's most popular sport?

ANSWERS

1. Atlantic Ocean
2. Cauto River
3. Turquino Peak
4. Sugarcane
5. Havana
6. Raúl Castro
7. Taíno
8. 1898
9. Esteban Bellán
10. Baseball

Key Words

amphibians: animals that live part of their lives in water and part on land

ancestors: parents, grandparents, or other family members who lived in an earlier time

architecture: the style in which buildings are designed

barrels: units of measure for oil equal to 42 gallons (159 liters)

cays: low islands of coral, rock, or sand

cobblestone: a round stone used to pave streets

colony: an area or country that is under the control of another country

communist: describes a system of government in which property and goods are owned by everyone in common

constitution: a written document stating a country's basic principles and laws

convert: to change beliefs, especially religious ones

dictator: a leader who has complete power and who may govern in a harsh or unfair way

emigrated: left one's country to live in another country or area

equator: an imaginary circle around Earth's surface that separates the Northern and Southern Hemispheres, or halves, of the planet

export: sale of products to another country

fertile: able to grow many plants easily

hydroelectricity: electricity produced using the energy of moving water

import: buy goods from another country

indigenous: native to a particular area

islets: little islands

life expectancy: the amount of time, on average, that a person in a certain population group can expect to live

mammals: warm-blooded animals that have hair or fur and nurse their young

mangrove: a tree or shrub that grows in swamps with salty water and that has roots partly above the ground

minerals: natural substances that are neither plants nor animals

plains: flat, treeless areas

plantations: big farms that are often worked by large numbers of people who live on the land

reptiles: cold-blooded animals, often covered with scales or plates, that lay eggs

reserves: resources still unused

species: groups of individuals with common characteristics

subsidizes: helps pay for the cost

UNESCO: the United Nations Educational, Scientific, and Cultural Organization, whose main goals are to promote world peace and eliminate poverty through education, science, and culture

Index

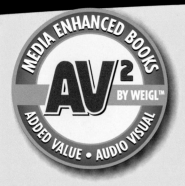

Log on to www.av2books.com

AV² by Weigl brings you media enhanced books that support active learning. Go to www.av2books.com, and enter the special code found on page 2 of this book. You will gain access to enriched and enhanced content that supplements and complements this book. Content includes video, audio, weblinks, quizzes, a slide show, and activities.

AV² Online Navigation

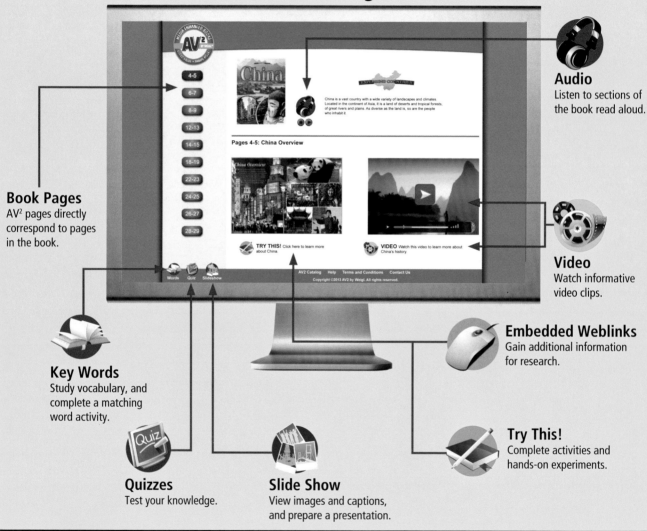

Audio
Listen to sections of the book read aloud.

Book Pages
AV² pages directly correspond to pages in the book.

Video
Watch informative video clips.

Embedded Weblinks
Gain additional information for research.

Key Words
Study vocabulary, and complete a matching word activity.

Try This!
Complete activities and hands-on experiments.

Quizzes
Test your knowledge.

Slide Show
View images and captions, and prepare a presentation.

AV² was built to bridge the gap between print and digital. We encourage you to tell us what you like and what you want to see in the future.

Sign up to be an AV² Ambassador at www.av2books.com/ambassador.